HOMEMAKER'S FRIEND

DAILY Planner

The 2017 Homemaker's Friend Daily Planner is dedicated to

Eldwin and Vera Rose Campbell

YOUR STEADY ENTHUSIASM IS GREATLY APPRECIATED.

SUE HOOLEY

An imprint of Christian Light Publications

2017 DAILY PLANNER

Christian Light Publications, Inc.
Harrisonburg, Virginia 22806

Printed in the United States of America.

13 Digit ISBN: 978-0-87813-789-3

To order planners by mail, please use order form in back.
Your comments and suggestions are welcomed!

Cover Design: Lanette Steiner
Text Design: Rhoda Miller & Lanette Steiner

A special note of thanks to Katherine Derstine
for choosing the Scripture verses.
The verses contain the theme of TIME.

HOLMES PRINTING SOLUTIONS
8757 County Road 77 . Fredericksburg, Ohio 44627 . 888.473.6870

THIS
Daily Planner
BELONGS TO:

_____

_____

_____

_____

IMPORTANT phone numbers:

Name: Phone:

_____   _____

_____   _____

_____   _____

_____   _____

_____   _____

_____   _____

_____   _____

_____   _____

_____   _____

2016

January 16
S	M	T	W	T	F	S
					1	2
3	4	5	6	7	8	9
10	11	12	13	14	15	16
17	18	19	20	21	22	23
24	25	26	27	28	29	30
31						

February 16
S	M	T	W	T	F	S
	1	2	3	4	5	6
7	8	9	10	11	12	13
14	15	16	17	18	19	20
21	22	23	24	25	26	27
28	29					

March 16
S	M	T	W	T	F	S
		1	2	3	4	5
6	7	8	9	10	11	12
13	14	15	16	17	18	19
20	21	22	23	24	25	26
27	28	29	30	31		

April 16
S	M	T	W	T	F	S
					1	2
3	4	5	6	7	8	9
10	11	12	13	14	15	16
17	18	19	20	21	22	23
24	25	26	27	28	29	30

May 16
S	M	T	W	T	F	S
1	2	3	4	5	6	7
8	9	10	11	12	13	14
15	16	17	18	19	20	21
22	23	24	25	26	27	28
29	30	31				

June 16
S	M	T	W	T	F	S
			1	2	3	4
5	6	7	8	9	10	11
12	13	14	15	16	17	18
19	20	21	22	23	24	25
26	27	28	29	30		

July 16
S	M	T	W	T	F	S
					1	2
3	4	5	6	7	8	9
10	11	12	13	14	15	16
17	18	19	20	21	22	23
24	25	26	27	28	29	30
31						

August 16
S	M	T	W	T	F	S
	1	2	3	4	5	6
7	8	9	10	11	12	13
14	15	16	17	18	19	20
21	22	23	24	25	26	27
28	29	30	31			

September 16
S	M	T	W	T	F	S
				1	2	3
4	5	6	7	8	9	10
11	12	13	14	15	16	17
18	19	20	21	22	23	24
25	26	27	28	29	30	

October 16
S	M	T	W	T	F	S
						1
2	3	4	5	6	7	8
9	10	11	12	13	14	15
16	17	18	19	20	21	22
23	24	25	26	27	28	29
30	31					

November 16
S	M	T	W	T	F	S
		1	2	3	4	5
6	7	8	9	10	11	12
13	14	15	16	17	18	19
20	21	22	23	24	25	26
27	28	29	30			

December 16
S	M	T	W	T	F	S
				1	2	3
4	5	6	7	8	9	10
11	12	13	14	15	16	17
18	19	20	21	22	23	24
25	26	27	28	29	30	31

2017

January 17
S	M	T	W	T	F	S
1	2	3	4	5	6	7
8	9	10	11	12	13	14
15	16	17	18	19	20	21
22	23	24	25	26	27	28
29	30	31				

February 17
S	M	T	W	T	F	S
			1	2	3	4
5	6	7	8	9	10	11
12	13	14	15	16	17	18
19	20	21	22	23	24	25
26	27	28				

March 17
S	M	T	W	T	F	S
			1	2	3	4
5	6	7	8	9	10	11
12	13	14	15	16	17	18
19	20	21	22	23	24	25
26	27	28	29	30	31	

April 17
S	M	T	W	T	F	S
						1
2	3	4	5	6	7	8
9	10	11	12	13	14	15
16	17	18	19	20	21	22
23	24	25	26	27	28	29
30						

May 17
S	M	T	W	T	F	S
	1	2	3	4	5	6
7	8	9	10	11	12	13
14	15	16	17	18	19	20
21	22	23	24	25	26	27
28	29	30	31			

June 17
S	M	T	W	T	F	S
				1	2	3
4	5	6	7	8	9	10
11	12	13	14	15	16	17
18	19	20	21	22	23	24
25	26	27	28	29	30	

July 17
S	M	T	W	T	F	S
						1
2	3	4	5	6	7	8
9	10	11	12	13	14	15
16	17	18	19	20	21	22
23	24	25	26	27	28	29
30	31					

August 17
S	M	T	W	T	F	S
		1	2	3	4	5
6	7	8	9	10	11	12
13	14	15	16	17	18	19
20	21	22	23	24	25	26
27	28	29	30	31		

September 17
S	M	T	W	T	F	S
					1	2
3	4	5	6	7	8	9
10	11	12	13	14	15	16
17	18	19	20	21	22	23
24	25	26	27	28	29	30

October 17
S	M	T	W	T	F	S
1	2	3	4	5	6	7
8	9	10	11	12	13	14
15	16	17	18	19	20	21
22	23	24	25	26	27	28
29	30	31				

November 17
S	M	T	W	T	F	S
			1	2	3	4
5	6	7	8	9	10	11
12	13	14	15	16	17	18
19	20	21	22	23	24	25
26	27	28	29	30		

December 17
S	M	T	W	T	F	S
					1	2
3	4	5	6	7	8	9
10	11	12	13	14	15	16
17	18	19	20	21	22	23
24	25	26	27	28	29	30
31						

2018

January 18
S	M	T	W	T	F	S
	1	2	3	4	5	6
7	8	9	10	11	12	13
14	15	16	17	18	19	20
21	22	23	24	25	26	27
28	29	30	31			

February 18
S	M	T	W	T	F	S
				1	2	3
4	5	6	7	8	9	10
11	12	13	14	15	16	17
18	19	20	21	22	23	24
25	26	27	28			

March 18
S	M	T	W	T	F	S
				1	2	3
4	5	6	7	8	9	10
11	12	13	14	15	16	17
18	19	20	21	22	23	24
25	26	27	28	29	30	31

April 18
S	M	T	W	T	F	S
1	2	3	4	5	6	7
8	9	10	11	12	13	14
15	16	17	18	19	20	21
22	23	24	25	26	27	28
29	30					

May 18
S	M	T	W	T	F	S
	1	2	3	4	5	
6	7	8	9	10	11	12
13	14	15	16	17	18	19
20	21	22	23	24	25	26
27	28	29	30	31		

June 18
S	M	T	W	T	F	S
					1	2
3	4	5	6	7	8	9
10	11	12	13	14	15	16
17	18	19	20	21	22	23
24	25	26	27	28	29	30

July 18
S	M	T	W	T	F	S
1	2	3	4	5	6	7
8	9	10	11	12	13	14
15	16	17	18	19	20	21
22	23	24	25	26	27	28
29	30	31				

August 18
S	M	T	W	T	F	S
			1	2	3	4
5	6	7	8	9	10	11
12	13	14	15	16	17	18
19	20	21	22	23	24	25
26	27	28	29	30	31	

September 18
S	M	T	W	T	F	S
						1
2	3	4	5	6	7	8
9	10	11	12	13	14	15
16	17	18	19	20	21	22
23	24	25	26	27	28	29
30						

October 18
S	M	T	W	T	F	S
	1	2	3	4	5	6
7	8	9	10	11	12	13
14	15	16	17	18	19	20
21	22	23	24	25	26	27
28	29	30	31			

November 18
S	M	T	W	T	F	S
				1	2	3
4	5	6	7	8	9	10
11	12	13	14	15	16	17
18	19	20	21	22	23	24
25	26	27	28	29	30	

December 18
S	M	T	W	T	F	S
						1
2	3	4	5	6	7	8
9	10	11	12	13	14	15
16	17	18	19	20	21	22
23	24	25	26	27	28	29
30	31					

2019

January 19
S	M	T	W	T	F	S
		1	2	3	4	5
6	7	8	9	10	11	12
13	14	15	16	17	18	19
20	21	22	23	24	25	26
27	28	29	30	31		

February 19
S	M	T	W	T	F	S
					1	2
3	4	5	6	7	8	9
10	11	12	13	14	15	16
17	18	19	20	21	22	23
24	25	26	27	28		

March 19
S	M	T	W	T	F	S
					1	2
3	4	5	6	7	8	9
10	11	12	13	14	15	16
17	18	19	20	21	22	23
24	25	26	27	28	29	30
31						

April 19
S	M	T	W	T	F	S
	1	2	3	4	5	6
7	8	9	10	11	12	13
14	15	16	17	18	19	20
21	22	23	24	25	26	27
28	29	30				

May 19
S	M	T	W	T	F	S
			1	2	3	4
5	6	7	8	9	10	11
12	13	14	15	16	17	18
19	20	21	22	23	24	25
26	27	28	29	30	31	

June 19
S	M	T	W	T	F	S
						1
2	3	4	5	6	7	8
9	10	11	12	13	14	15
16	17	18	19	20	21	22
23	24	25	26	27	28	29
30						

July 19
S	M	T	W	T	F	S
	1	2	3	4	5	6
7	8	9	10	11	12	13
14	15	16	17	18	19	20
21	22	23	24	25	26	27
28	29	30	31			

August 19
S	M	T	W	T	F	S
				1	2	3
4	5	6	7	8	9	10
11	12	13	14	15	16	17
18	19	20	21	22	23	24
25	26	27	28	29	30	31

September 19
S	M	T	W	T	F	S
1	2	3	4	5	6	7
8	9	10	11	12	13	14
15	16	17	18	19	20	21
22	23	24	25	26	27	28
29	30					

October 19
S	M	T	W	T	F	S
		1	2	3	4	5
6	7	8	9	10	11	12
13	14	15	16	17	18	19
20	21	22	23	24	25	26
27	28	29	30	31		

November 19
S	M	T	W	T	F	S
					1	2
3	4	5	6	7	8	9
10	11	12	13	14	15	16
17	18	19	20	21	22	23
24	25	26	27	28	29	30

December 19
S	M	T	W	T	F	S
1	2	3	4	5	6	7
8	9	10	11	12	13	14
15	16	17	18	19	20	21
22	23	24	25	26	27	28
29	30	31				

From the Pen of Sue...

Time Budgeting

You are probably familiar with a financial budget, but have you ever thought about a budget for time? Time and money are similar: both evaporate quickly without a plan. If a percentage of the pay check is not designated for monthly bills and we spend money impulsively, financial trouble will come. In the same way, if we use our time in a haphazard manner, eventually we feel overwhelmed and exhausted. A time budget is less meticulous than budgeting money, but an awareness of how you spend time will help you, even if you are not detailed.

How we manage our time can make the difference between a household in a continual upheaval and one that operates smoothly. In her book *Get More Done in Less Time*, Donna Otto suggests that you write down what you do in half-hour sections, for one week. She says, "Until you know exactly how you spend your time it is most difficult, in fact, near impossible, to reorganize."

Tracking Time

I took the challenge and the results made me question my mathematical skills. Did I actually spend thirteen hours talking on the telephone every week? It was a surprise that I spent ten hours running errands or making quick trips to town. I used up five hours going through the mail, and three different times I fried one pound of hamburger. Six mornings a week it took one hour to make beds and straighten up the house. I read for three hours and napped for six. Laundry took about twelve hours. At that time, I had three children under age six, so much of my time was spent on child care.

As the week progressed, it was obvious that I was squandering time. *Could it be possible that only a few changes might lessen my feeling of being constantly overwhelmed?* A flicker of hope surfaced as new ideas began formulating. It took time to develop new habits, but after discovering where my time was going and making adjustments, my feeling of overload began to dissipate.

When budgeting time, learn to think of a day in sections, such as morning, afternoon, and evening. Since Sunday is a day of rest, we have six workdays, giving us a total of eighteen sections in a week. We can often accomplish more if we think of our work in terms of those sections.

Perhaps you will spend a morning taking care of mail or phone calls, and in the afternoon you might make cookies or take a nap. Interruptions *will* come and scheduling the day too full will cause frustration. Be flexible when planning activities and always take into consideration the stage of your family.

As the stages of life may change, we can adjust the titles of our time sections. If you are a mom of preschoolers, the divisions may be morning, naptime, and before supper. Evenings may be as varied as your husband's occupation. It is important to learn where the pockets of time are and how to make the best use of them.

Making Time Work for You

Some jobs can easily be done in several hours, but many projects are too large to neatly fit into small portions of time. Time budgeting can help us arrange our activities so we can find a larger space of workable time.

These larger projects are not regular weekly tasks, but things you must eventually complete. For example, you may need to organize your recipes, get ready for a family reunion, or paint the living room. Keeping a master list of things you need to do will give a picture of projects on the horizon.

First, consider on which day of the week you have the least number of demands. Generally, I do laundry on Monday, Thursday, and Saturday. Wednesday evening, we attend a midweek church service. I often clean the house on Friday and get ready for the weekend. Tuesday is the only day of the week that does not involve duties beyond normal living.

Planning projects in advance helps you to have the necessary tools on hand. Eliminating a special trip to town for supplies will save you time and money. In addition, your work flow will not be interrupted; therefore, you gain minutes of prime working time.

When planning a project for a "Tuesday," (or your day of choice) perhaps you could find a slot of time in advance for preparation. This will boost your productivity. For example, if you plan to work on a craft, gather supplies the day before. If your household is like mine, it might take thirty minutes to locate the hot glue gun and an extension cord.

A day set aside may need to be guarded carefully. If possible, schedule appointments on other days. An 11:00 dentist appointment will take a huge chunk of valuable time or you may need to say, "Thanks for asking, but it really doesn't suit me to meet for coffee." However, we must be flexible so that we are able to recognize Divine arrangements.

Be creative in finding ways to keep your children entertained. If you spend a few minutes helping them get started with an activity, they are more likely to play happily. Children will not feel neglected if you have given some thought to making their day special. It can be done discreetly so they may not even realize that you are extra busy or that you are trying to keep them entertained. For example, when my older children were young, if I wanted to do a thinking job or an involving one, I'd maybe play a game with them first or read a few stories, and then drape a blanket over the table, pack their lunch in a brown bag and hide it outside, or something else special to occupy them while I worked. I kept some toys separate from the others—they weren't really that great, but the children could only play with those toys with permission. To this day we still have several boxes labeled "Special toys."

If a project doesn't get completed on a "Tuesday," sometimes it can roll over to the next day. However, depending on the type of project, it may be best to set it aside even if you aren't finished, especially if the remainder of the week is full.

Take care that you do not overload your schedule. In spite of the bigger projects that need to be done, normal household duties still exist. The general household can deteriorate quickly when we are working on a time-consuming project. If you spend a large amount of time on a project one week, perhaps the next week should be less intense so you can catch up on neglected duties. We owe it to our families to create a homey stress-free atmosphere. While sometimes it is alright to let things slide, it isn't healthy over the long-term.

A project day is not always about getting work done. If it seldom snows in your area, don't miss the chance to build a snowman just because it is a "Tuesday." All households experience spur-of-the-moment opportunities. Be flexible so you can make the best of these occasions. Sometimes a "Tuesday" is an excellent time to plan a fun day with the children. If you wait until you "have enough time" you may miss the chance to invest in memory-making events.

Time budgeting is not about increasing your work load. Rather it is about helping you arrange your activities efficiently to give you freedom to do other important things. You may have time to take flowers to an ailing neighbor. Perhaps you will be in a better frame of mind when your husband comes home from work. You may have time to enjoy a cup of coffee and read a book for the simple pleasure it gives.

At first, budgeting time may feel like a great deal of extra work, but soon you will realize that it is an advantage. The more you work at budgeting your time, the better you will become at it and you will feel less overwhelmed. Time is a gift. As we budget it wisely, it will yield returns of greater peace and more flexibility.

"When work is a pleasure, life is a joy!
When work is a duty, life is slavery."
-Maxim Gorky

The Daily Planner was designed by Sue Hooley, wife of Dan for 26 years and mother to six children, two girls and four boys ages 7-23. The planner was developed after several years of motherhood and homemaking. Sue understood that a homemaker's day can rarely be scheduled and structured the same as the one before, nor can every task fit neatly into the timeslot allotted by other planners. Since her first publication in 2010, thousands of homemakers have benefited from the Daily Planner.

If you have comments about the Daily Planner, you may share your thoughts by sending an e-mail to: sue@homemakersfriend.com
or writing to: Sue Hooley 3176A Bulldog Creek Road, Valley, WA 99181.
To read more, visit www.homemakersdepot.com

If you like this planner, help us out by leaving a review on Amazon.

THE HOMEMAKER'S FRIEND
Daily Planner

The Homemaker's Friend Daily Planner is divided into the following seven sections:

YEARLY CALENDAR. This is for jotting down upcoming events, or making note of a special happening. The additional pages include 52 sections—one for each week. Homemaker's Friend Planner users asked for these additional pages on which to journal or write prayer requests, birthdays, and quotes.

MONTHLY CALENDAR. Record upcoming events such as church meetings, weddings, school activities, appointments, reunions, and holidays. This becomes useful for weekly scheduling because you can see at a glance what will be happening over the next several months.

WEEKLY PLANNING. Under the heading *Tasks List* are spaces to jot down specific duties you want to accomplish—phone calls, appointments, balancing the checkbook, and so on.

It's beneficial to take time to sketch out weekly tasks in advance. If a dentist appointment needs to be scheduled, write it down. If laundry is the biggest event on Monday, write it down. Look for short slots of time to do small projects. It only takes a few minutes to schedule a dentist appointment or to send a card and if it is written down, you are more apt to grab those precious few minutes when the opportunity arises. If a suit needs to be taken to the dry cleaners, jot it down so it isn't forgotten on the next trip to town. The *shaded area* to the right of the day of the week is a place to write birthdays or weekly reminders. The *menu block* is for the main meal of the day.

To make the current weekly layout easy to find, clip the top corner of the page on the *dotted line*. If you write with a pencil, daily tasks can easily be erased and rearranged to accommodate the unpredicted issues that come along.

TASKS LIST. The pages in this section are untitled, allowing you the freedom to create monthly, bi-monthly or seasonal lists. If you do a lot of gardening and food preservation, title the page *Summer Projects*. Then make a list of things you want to freeze or preserve. As each food project is completed, you can enjoy the pleasure of crossing it off the list.

PROJECTS AND EVENTS. The *Projects and Events* section is for occasions that need more space for writing. If planning a baby shower or a family gathering, keep that information in your planner for quick reference. These pages are untitled for flexibility.

INFORMATION. Use this section for phone numbers and addresses needed temporarily. For example, when placing an order, jot down the number so you won't need to look it up again. This is a good place to write addresses for a card shower or the information for the eye specialist.

SHOPPING LISTS. These may be used as comprehensive shopping lists or as a central location to write the items needed for upcoming events, projects, or menus. A running shopping list helps to make the best of a trip to town, whether it is planned or unexpected. The lists are perforated for your convenience.

The pages following the shopping lists offer a place to write clothing sizes, gift ideas, and item checklists. Two customizable master shopping lists are included—one for a practice sheet and the other for a final list. The checklist pages are for particular stores. For example, if there are items you usually purchase at Costco, this checklist can serve as a reminder.

CONSULT YOUR PLANNER OFTEN. At first it may feel stiff like a new shoe, but the more you use it, the more it will feel like a friend. When scheduling, balance home responsibilities with other obligations to create a realistic schedule that is best *just for today*. It is typical to veer from a daily plan when urgent matters arise, but a written plan will refresh your memory and keep your focus on what is most important.

Yearly
CALENDAR

NOTES

WHEN TIME
is spent,
Eternity
BEGINS.

HELEN HUNT JACKSON

2017 Mini Calendars

January

S	M	T	W	T	F	S
1	2	3	4	5	6	7
8	9	10	11	12	13	14
15	16	17	18	19	20	21
22	23	24	25	26	27	28
29	30	31				

February

S	M	T	W	T	F	S
			1	2	3	4
5	6	7	8	9	10	11
12	13	14	15	16	17	18
19	20	21	22	23	24	25
26	27	28				

March

S	M	T	W	T	F	S
			1	2	3	4
5	6	7	8	9	10	11
12	13	14	15	16	17	18
19	20	21	22	23	24	25
26	27	28	29	30	31	

April

S	M	T	W	T	F	S
						1
2	3	4	5	6	7	8
9	10	11	12	13	14	15
16	17	18	19	20	21	22
23 30	24	25	26	27	28	29

May

S	M	T	W	T	F	S
	1	2	3	4	5	6
7	8	9	10	11	12	13
14	15	16	17	18	19	20
21	22	23	24	25	26	27
28	29	30	31			

June

S	M	T	W	T	F	S
				1	2	3
4	5	6	7	8	9	10
11	12	13	14	15	16	17
18	19	20	21	22	23	24
25	26	27	28	29	30	

July

S	M	T	W	T	F	S
						1
2	3	4	5	6	7	8
9	10	11	12	13	14	15
16	17	18	19	20	21	22
23 30	24 31	25	26	27	28	29

August

S	M	T	W	T	F	S
		1	2	3	4	5
6	7	8	9	10	11	12
13	14	15	16	17	18	19
20	21	22	23	24	25	26
27	28	29	30	31		

September

S	M	T	W	T	F	S
					1	2
3	4	5	6	7	8	9
10	11	12	13	14	15	16
17	18	19	20	21	22	23
24	25	26	27	28	29	30

October

S	M	T	W	T	F	S
1	2	3	4	5	6	7
8	9	10	11	12	13	14
15	16	17	18	19	20	21
22	23	24	25	26	27	28
29	30	31				

November

S	M	T	W	T	F	S
			1	2	3	4
5	6	7	8	9	10	11
12	13	14	15	16	17	18
19	20	21	22	23	24	25
26	27	28	29	30		

December

S	M	T	W	T	F	S
					1	2
3	4	5	6	7	8	9
10	11	12	13	14	15	16
17	18	19	20	21	22	23
24 31	25	26	27	28	29	30

2017 Dates to Remember

January

_____
_____
_____
_____
_____

February

_____
_____
_____
_____
_____

March

_____
_____
_____
_____
_____

April

_____
_____
_____
_____
_____

May

_____
_____
_____
_____
_____

June

_____
_____
_____
_____
_____

July

_____
_____
_____
_____
_____

August

_____
_____
_____
_____
_____

September

_____
_____
_____
_____
_____

October

_____
_____
_____
_____
_____

November

_____
_____
_____
_____
_____

December

_____
_____
_____
_____
_____

2018 Mini Calendars

January
S	M	T	W	T	F	S
	1	2	3	4	5	6
7	8	9	10	11	12	13
14	15	16	17	18	19	20
21	22	23	24	25	26	27
28	29	30	31			

February
S	M	T	W	T	F	S
				1	2	3
4	5	6	7	8	9	10
11	12	13	14	15	16	17
18	19	20	21	22	23	24
25	26	27	28			

March
S	M	T	W	T	F	S
				1	2	3
4	5	6	7	8	9	10
11	12	13	14	15	16	17
18	19	20	21	22	23	24
25	26	27	28	29	30	31

April
S	M	T	W	T	F	S
1	2	3	4	5	6	7
8	9	10	11	12	13	14
15	16	17	18	19	20	21
22	23	24	25	26	27	28
29	30					

May
S	M	T	W	T	F	S
		1	2	3	4	5
6	7	8	9	10	11	12
13	14	15	16	17	18	19
20	21	22	23	24	25	26
27	28	29	30	31		

June
S	M	T	W	T	F	S
					1	2
3	4	5	6	7	8	9
10	11	12	13	14	15	16
17	18	19	20	21	22	23
24	25	26	27	28	29	30

July
S	M	T	W	T	F	S
1	2	3	4	5	6	7
8	9	10	11	12	13	14
15	16	17	18	19	20	21
22	23	24	25	26	27	28
29	30	31				

August
S	M	T	W	T	F	S
			1	2	3	4
5	6	7	8	9	10	11
12	13	14	15	16	17	18
19	20	21	22	23	24	25
26	27	28	29	30	31	

September
S	M	T	W	T	F	S
						1
2	3	4	5	6	7	8
9	10	11	12	13	14	15
16	17	18	19	20	21	22
23 30	24	25	26	27	28	29

October
S	M	T	W	T	F	S
	1	2	3	4	5	6
7	8	9	10	11	12	13
14	15	16	17	18	19	20
21	22	23	24	25	26	27
28	29	30	31			

November
S	M	T	W	T	F	S
				1	2	3
4	5	6	7	8	9	10
11	12	13	14	15	16	17
18	19	20	21	22	23	24
25	26	27	28	29	30	

December
S	M	T	W	T	F	S
						1
2	3	4	5	6	7	8
9	10	11	12	13	14	15
16	17	18	19	20	21	22
23 30	24 31	25	26	27	28	29

2018 Dates to Remember

January

February

March

April

May

June

July

August

September

October

November

December

Monthly
CALENDAR

NOTES

Only God
can turn a *mess* into a *message*,
A TEST INTO A TESTIMONY,
a trial *into a* triumph,
AND A VICTIM INTO A VICTORY.

January 2017

SUNDAY	MONDAY	TUESDAY
1 New Year's Day	2	3
8	9	10
15	16 Martin Luther King Jr. Day	17
22	23	24
29	30	31

December 2016						
S	M	T	W	T	F	S
				1	2	3
4	5	6	7	8	9	10
11	12	13	14	15	16	17
18	19	20	21	22	23	24
25	26	27	28	29	30	31

February						
S	M	T	W	T	F	S
			1	2	3	4
5	6	7	8	9	10	11
12	13	14	15	16	17	18
19	20	21	22	23	24	25
26	27	28				

WEDNESDAY	THURSDAY	FRIDAY	SATURDAY
4	5	6	7
11	12	13	14
18	19	20	21
25	26	27	28

Cut along dotted line to expose tabs.

February 2017

NOTES

SUNDAY	MONDAY	TUESDAY
5	6	7
12	13	14 Valentine's Day
19	20 Presidents' Day	21
26	27	28

	January					
S	M	T	W	T	F	S
1	2	3	4	5	6	7
8	9	10	11	12	13	14
15	16	17	18	19	20	21
22	23	24	25	26	27	28
29	30	31				

	March					
S	M	T	W	T	F	S
			1	2	3	4
5	6	7	8	9	10	11
12	13	14	15	16	17	18
19	20	21	22	23	24	25
26	27	28	29	30	31	

WEDNESDAY	THURSDAY	FRIDAY	SATURDAY
1	2	3	4
	Groundhog Day		
8	9	10	11
15	16	17	18
22	23	24	25

Cut along dotted line to expose tabs.

March 2017

SUNDAY	MONDAY	TUESDAY
5	6	7
12 Daylight Saving Time Begins	13	14
19	20	21
26	27	28

February

S	M	T	W	T	F	S
			1	2	3	4
5	6	7	8	9	10	11
12	13	14	15	16	17	18
19	20	21	22	23	24	25
26	27	28				

April

S	M	T	W	T	F	S
						1
2	3	4	5	6	7	8
9	10	11	12	13	14	15
16	17	18	19	20	21	22
23	24	25	26	27	28	29
30						

WEDNESDAY	THURSDAY	FRIDAY	SATURDAY
1 Ash Wednesday	2	3	4
8	9	10	11
15	16	17 St. Patrick's Day	18
22	23	24	25
29	30	31	

Cut along dotted line to expose tabs.

April 2017

SUNDAY	MONDAY	TUESDAY
2	3	4
9	10	11
Palm Sunday		
16	17	18
Easter		
23 30	24	25

	March					
S	M	T	W	T	F	S
			1	2	3	4
5	6	7	8	9	10	11
12	13	14	15	16	17	18
19	20	21	22	23	24	25
26	27	28	29	30	31	

	May					
S	M	T	W	T	F	S
	1	2	3	4	5	6
7	8	9	10	11	12	13
14	15	16	17	18	19	20
21	22	23	24	25	26	27
28	29	30	31			

Apr.

Cut along dotted line to expose tabs.

WEDNESDAY	THURSDAY	FRIDAY	SATURDAY
			1
5	6	7	8
12	13	14 Good Friday	15
19	20	21	22
26	27	28	29

XII

VI

May 2017

SUNDAY	MONDAY	TUESDAY
	1	2
7	8	9
14 Mother's Day	15	16
21	22	23
28	29 Memorial Day	30

April

S	M	T	W	T	F	S
						1
2	3	4	5	6	7	8
9	10	11	12	13	14	15
16	17	18	19	20	21	22
23	24	25	26	27	28	29
30						

June

S	M	T	W	T	F	S
				1	2	3
4	5	6	7	8	9	10
11	12	13	14	15	16	17
18	19	20	21	22	23	24
25	26	27	28	29	30	

WEDNESDAY	THURSDAY	FRIDAY	SATURDAY
3	4	5	6
10	11	12	13
17	18	19	20
24	25	26	27
31			

May

Cut along dotted line to expose tabs.

June 2017

SUNDAY	MONDAY	TUESDAY
4	5	6
11	12	13
18	19	20
Father's Day		
25	26	27

		May								*July*			
S	M	T	W	T	F	S	S	M	T	W	T	F	S
	1	2	3	4	5	6							1
7	8	9	10	11	12	13	2	3	4	5	6	7	8
14	15	16	17	18	19	20	9	10	11	12	13	14	15
21	22	23	24	25	26	27	16	17	18	19	20	21	22
28	29	30	31				23	24	25	26	27	28	29
							30	31					

WEDNESDAY	THURSDAY	FRIDAY	SATURDAY
	1	2	3
7	8	9	10
14	15	16	17
21 *Sam Stoltzfus 12:00*	22 *Martha Brubacher 8:30* / *Carolyn 2:15*	23 *Green Dragon 5:30* / *Abbot comes*	24 *Feed Jane's Cats*
28	29	30	

June

Cut along dotted line to expose tabs.

July 2017

SUNDAY	MONDAY	TUESDAY
2	3	4 Independence Day
9	10	11
16	17	18
23 30	24 31	25

June						
S	M	T	W	T	F	S
				1	2	3
4	5	6	7	8	9	10
11	12	13	14	15	16	17
18	19	20	21	22	23	24
25	26	27	28	29	30	

August						
S	M	T	W	T	F	S
		1	2	3	4	5
6	7	8	9	10	11	12
13	14	15	16	17	18	19
20	21	22	23	24	25	26
27	28	29	30	31		

WEDNESDAY	THURSDAY	FRIDAY	SATURDAY
			1
5	6	7	8
12	13	14	15
19	20	21	22
26	27	28	29

July

Cut along dotted line to expose tabs.

August 2017

SUNDAY	MONDAY	TUESDAY
		1
6	7	8
13	14	15
20	21	22
27	28	29

NOTES

July

S	M	T	W	T	F	S
						1
2	3	4	5	6	7	8
9	10	11	12	13	14	15
16	17	18	19	20	21	22
23	24	25	26	27	28	29
30	31					

September

S	M	T	W	T	F	S
					1	2
3	4	5	6	7	8	9
10	11	12	13	14	15	16
17	18	19	20	21	22	23
24	25	26	27	28	29	30

WEDNESDAY	THURSDAY	FRIDAY	SATURDAY
2	3	4	5
9	10	11	12
16	17	18	19
23	24	25	26
30	31		

Aug.

XII

VI

Cut along dotted line to expose tabs.

September 2017

SUNDAY	MONDAY	TUESDAY
3	4	5
	Labor Day	
10	11	12
17	18	19
24	25	26

NOTES

	August					
S	M	T	W	T	F	S
		1	2	3	4	5
6	7	8	9	10	11	12
13	14	15	16	17	18	19
20	21	22	23	24	25	26
27	28	29	30	31		

	October					
S	M	T	W	T	F	S
1	2	3	4	5	6	7
8	9	10	11	12	13	14
15	16	17	18	19	20	21
22	23	24	25	26	27	28
29	30	31				

WEDNESDAY	THURSDAY	FRIDAY	SATURDAY
		1	2
6	7	8	9
13	14	15	16
20	21	22	23
27	28	29	30

Sept.

Cut along dotted line to expose tabs.

October 2017

SUNDAY	MONDAY	TUESDAY
1	2	3
8	9 Columbus Day	10
15	16	17
22	23	24
29	30	31

	September					
S	M	T	W	T	F	S
					1	2
3	4	5	6	7	8	9
10	11	12	13	14	15	16
17	18	19	20	21	22	23
24	25	26	27	28	29	30

	November					
S	M	T	W	T	F	S
			1	2	3	4
5	6	7	8	9	10	11
12	13	14	15	16	17	18
19	20	21	22	23	24	25
26	27	28	29	30		

WEDNESDAY	THURSDAY	FRIDAY	SATURDAY
4	5	6	7
11	12	13	14
18	19	20	21
25	26	27	28

Oct.

XII

VI

November 2017

SUNDAY	MONDAY	TUESDAY
5 Daylight Saving Time Ends	6	7
12	13	14
19	20	21
26	27	28

NOTES

October

S	M	T	W	T	F	S
	1	2	3	4	5	6	7
8	9	10	11	12	13	14
15	16	17	18	19	20	21
22	23	24	25	26	27	28
29	30	31				

December

S	M	T	W	T	F	S
					1	2
3	4	5	6	7	8	9
10	11	12	13	14	15	16
17	18	19	20	21	22	23
24	25	26	27	28	29	30
31						

WEDNESDAY	THURSDAY	FRIDAY	SATURDAY
1	2	3	4
8	9	10	11 Veteran's Day
15	16	17	18
22	23 Thanksgiving	24	25
29	30		

Nov.

December 2017

SUNDAY	MONDAY	TUESDAY
3	4	5
10	11	12
17	18	19
24 / 31 — Christmas Eve / New Year's Eve	25 — Christmas	26

November

S	M	T	W	T	F	S
			1	2	3	4
5	6	7	8	9	10	11
12	13	14	15	16	17	18
19	20	21	22	23	24	25
26	27	28	29	30		

January 2018

S	M	T	W	T	F	S
	1	2	3	4	5	6
7	8	9	10	11	12	13
14	15	16	17	18	19	20
21	22	23	24	25	26	27
28	29	30	31			

WEDNESDAY	THURSDAY	FRIDAY	SATURDAY
		1	2
6	7	8	9
13	14	15	16
20	21	22	23
27	28	29	30

Dec.

NOTES

Weekly
PLANNING

NOTES

NO ACT
OF
kindness
no matter how small,
IS EVER WASTED.

AESOP

TASKS LIST

Dec. 5, 2016 - Dec. 11, 2016

But the salvation of the righteous is
of the LORD: he is their strength in
the time of trouble.
PSALM 37:39

				1	2	3
4	5	6	7	8	9	10
11	12	13	14	15	16	17
18	19	20	21	22	23	24
25	26	27	28	29	30	31

December

MONDAY 5

Menu:

TUESDAY 6

Menu:

Cut here

WEDNESDAY 7

Menu:

THURSDAY 8

Menu:

FRIDAY 9

Menu:

SATURDAY 10

Menu:

SUNDAY 11

Menu:

TASKS LIST

Trust in him at all times; ye
people, pour out your heart before
him: God is a refuge for us. Selah.
PSALM 62:8

December						
				1	2	3
4	5	6	7	8	9	10
11	12	13	14	15	16	17
18	19	20	21	22	23	24
25	26	27	28	29	30	31

MONDAY 12

Menu:

TUESDAY 13

Menu:

WEDNESDAY 14

Menu:

THURSDAY 15

Menu:

FRIDAY 16

Menu:

SATURDAY 17

Menu:

SUNDAY 18

Menu:

TASKS LIST

Dec. 19, 2016 - Dec. 25, 2016

Thou, O LORD, remainest for ever;
thy throne from generation to
generation.
LAMENTATIONS 5:19

December

				1	2	3
4	5	6	7	8	9	10
11	12	13	14	15	16	17
18	19	20	21	22	23	24
25	26	27	28	29	30	31

MONDAY 19

Menu:

TUESDAY 20

Menu:

Cut here

WEDNESDAY 21

Menu:

THURSDAY 22

Menu:

FRIDAY 23

Menu:

SATURDAY 24

Menu:

SUNDAY 25

CHRISTMAS DAY

Menu:

TASKS LIST

So teach us to number our days,
that we may apply our hearts unto
wisdom.

PSALM 90:12

					1	2	3
4	5	6	7	8	9	10	
11	12	13	14	15	16	17	
18	19	20	21	22	23	24	
25	26	27	28	29	30	31	
1	2	3	4	5	6	7	

December

MONDAY 26

CHRISTMAS DAY OBSERVED

Menu:

TUESDAY 27

Menu:

Cut here

WEDNESDAY 28

Menu:

THURSDAY 29

Menu:

FRIDAY 30

Menu:

SATURDAY 31

SUNDAY 1

NEW YEAR'S EVE

NEW YEAR'S DAY

Menu:

Menu:

TASKS LIST

Jan. 2 - Jan. 8

I said, Days should speak, and
multitude of years should teach
wisdom.
JOB 32:7

1	2	3	4	5	6	7	
8	9	10	11	12	13	14	January
15	16	17	18	19	20	21	
22	23	24	25	26	27	28	
29	30	31					

MONDAY 2

Menu:

TUESDAY 3

Menu:

Cut here

WEDNESDAY 4

Menu:

THURSDAY 5

Menu:

FRIDAY 6

Menu:

SATURDAY 7

Menu:

SUNDAY 8

Menu:

TASKS LIST

Jan. 9 - Jan. 15

The counsel of the LORD standeth for
ever, the thoughts of his heart to all
generations.
PSALM 33:11

January						
1	2	3	4	5	6	7
8	9	10	11	12	13	14
15	16	17	18	19	20	21
22	23	24	25	26	27	28
29	30	31				

MONDAY 9

Menu:

TUESDAY 10

Menu:

WEDNESDAY 11

Menu:

THURSDAY 12

Menu:

FRIDAY 13

Menu:

SATURDAY 14

SUNDAY 15

Menu:

Menu:

TASKS LIST

Jan. 16 - Jan. 22

I must work the works of him that sent
me, while it is day: the night cometh,
when no man can work.
JOHN 9:4

	1	2	3	4	5	6	7	
	8	9	10	11	12	13	14	January
	15	16	17	18	19	20	21	
	22	23	24	25	26	27	28	
	29	30	31					

MONDAY 16

MARTIN LUTHER KING JR. DAY

Menu:

TUESDAY 17

Menu:

WEDNESDAY 18

Menu:

THURSDAY 19

Menu:

FRIDAY 20

Menu:

SATURDAY 21

SUNDAY 22

Menu:

Menu:

TASKS LIST

Jan. 23 - Jan. 29

For he that will love life, and see good
days, let him refrain his tongue from evil,
and his lips that they speak no guile.
1 PETER 3:10

							January
1	2	3	4	5	6	7
8	9	10	11	12	13	14
15	16	17	18	19	20	21
22	23	24	25	26	27	28
29	30	31				

MONDAY 23

Menu:

TUESDAY 24

Menu:

Cut here

WEDNESDAY 25

Menu:

THURSDAY 26

Menu:

FRIDAY 27

Menu:

SATURDAY 28

Menu:

SUNDAY 29

Menu:

TASKS LIST

Jan. 30 - Feb. 5

A time to get, and a time to lose; a time
to keep, and a time to cast away.
ECCLESIASTES 3:6

1	2	3	4	5	6	7	
8	9	10	11	12	13	14	*January*
15	16	17	18	19	20	21	
22	23	24	25	26	27	28	
29	30	31	*1*	*2*	*3*	*4*	
5							

MONDAY 30

Menu:

TUESDAY 31

Menu:

WEDNESDAY 1

Menu:

THURSDAY 2

GROUNDHOG DAY

Menu:

FRIDAY 3

Menu:

SATURDAY 4

Menu:

SUNDAY 5

Menu:

TASKS LIST

WEEK: 6

Feb. 6 - Feb. 12

O satisfy us early with thy mercy; that we may rejoice and be glad all our days.
PSALM 90:14

			1	2	3	4	February
5	6	7	8	9	10	11	
12	13	14	15	16	17	18	
19	20	21	22	23	24	25	
26	27	28					

MONDAY 6

Menu:

TUESDAY 7

Menu:

WEDNESDAY 8

Menu:

THURSDAY 9

Menu:

FRIDAY 10

Menu:

SATURDAY 11

SUNDAY 12

Menu:

Menu:

Cut here

TASKS LIST

Feb. 13 - Feb. 19

Before the mountains were brought forth, or ever
thou hadst formed the earth and the world, even
from everlasting to everlasting, thou art God.
PSALM 90:2

			1	2	3	4	*February*
5	6	7	8	9	10	11	
12	13	14	15	16	17	18	
19	20	21	22	23	24	25	
26	27	28					

MONDAY 13

Menu:

TUESDAY 14

VALENTINE'S DAY

Menu:

Cut here

WEDNESDAY 15

Menu:

THURSDAY 16

Menu:

FRIDAY 17

Menu:

SATURDAY 18

Menu:

SUNDAY 19

Menu:

TASKS LIST

Feb. 20 - Feb. 26

A time to rend, and a time to sew; a time
to keep silence, and a time to speak.
ECCLESIASTES 3:7

				1	2	3	4
5	6	7	8	9	10	11
12	13	14	15	16	17	18
19	20	21	22	23	24	25
26	27	28

February

MONDAY 20

PRESIDENTS' DAY

Menu:

TUESDAY 21

Menu:

WEDNESDAY 22

Menu:

THURSDAY 23

Menu:

FRIDAY 24

Menu:

SATURDAY 25

Menu:

SUNDAY 26

Menu:

Cut here

TASKS LIST

Feb. 27 - Mar. 5

And even to your old age I am he; and even
to hoar hairs will I carry you: I have made,
and I will bear; even I will carry, and will
deliver you.
ISAIAH 46:4

			1	2	3	4
5	6	7	8	9	10	11
12	13	14	15	16	17	18
19	20	21	22	23	24	25
26	27	28	1	2	3	4
5						

February

MONDAY 27

Menu:

TUESDAY 28

Menu:

WEDNESDAY 1

ASH WEDNESDAY

Menu:

THURSDAY 2

Menu:

FRIDAY 3

Menu:

SATURDAY 4

Menu:

SUNDAY 5

Menu:

TASKS LIST

Mar. 6 - Mar. 12

When a few years are come, then I shall go
the way whence I shall not return.
JOB 16:22

				1	2	3	4	*March*
5	6	7	8	9	10	11
12	13	14	15	16	17	18
19	20	21	22	23	24	25
26	27	28	29	30	31

MONDAY 6

Menu:

TUESDAY 7

Menu:

WEDNESDAY 8

Menu:

THURSDAY 9

Menu:

FRIDAY 10

Menu:

SATURDAY 11

Menu:

SUNDAY 12

DAYLIGHT SAVINGS TIME BEGINS

Menu:

TASKS LIST

Mar. 13 - Mar. 19

And that, knowing the time, that now it is
high time to awake out of sleep: for now is
our salvation nearer than when we believed.
ROMANS 13:11

				1	2	3	4
5	6	7	8	9	10	11
12	13	14	15	16	17	18
19	20	21	22	23	24	25
26	27	28	29	30	31	

MONDAY 13

Menu:

TUESDAY 14

Menu:

WEDNESDAY 15

Menu:

THURSDAY 16

Menu:

FRIDAY 17

ST. PATRICK'S DAY

Menu:

SATURDAY 18

SUNDAY 19

Menu:

Menu:

Cut here

TASKS LIST

Mar. 20 - Mar. 26

To every thing there is a season,
and a time to every purpose under
the heaven.
ECCLESIASTES 3:1

March

			1	2	3	4
5	6	7	8	9	10	11
12	13	14	15	16	17	18
19	20	21	22	23	24	25
26	27	28	29	30	31	

MONDAY 20

	Menu:

TUESDAY 21

	Menu:

WEDNESDAY 22

Menu:

THURSDAY 23

Menu:

FRIDAY 24

Menu:

SATURDAY 25

SUNDAY 26

Menu:

Menu:

TASKS LIST

Mar. 27 - Apr. 2

Behold, God is great, and we know
him not, neither can the number of his
years be searched out.
JOB 36:26

				1	2	3	4	*March*
5	6	7	8	9	10	11
12	13	14	15	16	17	18
19	20	21	22	23	24	25
26	27	28	29	30	31	*1*
2						

MONDAY 27

Menu:

TUESDAY 28

Menu:

WEDNESDAY 29

Menu:

THURSDAY 30

Menu:

FRIDAY 31

Menu:

SATURDAY 1

Menu:

SUNDAY 2

Menu:

TASKS LIST

Apr. 3 - Apr. 9

For which cause we faint not; but though
our outward man perish, yet the inward
man is renewed day by day.
2 CORINTHIANS 4:16

						1
2	3	4	5	6	7	8
9	10	11	12	13	14	15
16	17	18	19	20	21	22
23	24	25	26	27	28	29
30						

April

MONDAY 3

Menu:

TUESDAY 4

Menu:

WEDNESDAY 5

Menu:

THURSDAY 6

Menu:

FRIDAY 7

Menu:

SATURDAY 8

Menu:

SUNDAY 9

PALM SUNDAY

Menu:

Cut here

TASKS LIST

WEEK: 15

Apr. 10 - Apr. 16

And that he was buried, and that he rose
again the third day according to the
scriptures.
1 CORINTHIANS 15:4

	April
	1
2 3 4 5 6 7	8
9 10 11 12 13 14	15
16 17 18 19 20 21	22
23 24 25 26 27 28	29
30	

MONDAY 10

Menu:

TUESDAY 11

Menu:

WEDNESDAY 12

Menu:

THURSDAY 13

Menu:

FRIDAY 14

GOOD FRIDAY

Menu:

SATURDAY 15

SUNDAY 16

EASTER

Menu:

Menu:

T A S K S   L I S T

Apr. 17 - Apr. 23

As for man, his days are as grass: as a flower
of the field, so he flourisheth. For the wind
passeth over it, and it is gone; and the place
thereof shall know it no more.
PSALM 103:15,16

April

						1
2	3	4	5	6	7	8
9	10	11	12	13	14	15
16	17	18	19	20	21	22
23	24	25	26	27	28	29
30						

MONDAY 17

Menu:

TUESDAY 18

Menu:

WEDNESDAY 19

Menu:

THURSDAY 20

Menu:

FRIDAY 21

Menu:

SATURDAY 22

Menu:

SUNDAY 23

Menu:

TASKS LIST

Apr. 24 - Apr. 30

Take ye heed, watch and pray:
for ye know not when the time is.
MARK 13:33

						1
2	3	4	5	6	7	8
9	10	11	12	13	14	15
16	17	18	19	20	21	22
23	24	25	26	27	28	29
30						

April

MONDAY 24

Menu:

TUESDAY 25

Menu:

WEDNESDAY 26

Menu:

THURSDAY 27

Menu:

FRIDAY 28

Menu:

SATURDAY 29

Menu:

SUNDAY 30

Menu:

TASKS LIST

May 1 - May 7

In the morning sow thy seed, and in the evening
withhold not thine hand: for thou knowest not
whether shall prosper, either this or that, or
whether they both shall be alike good.
ECCLESIASTES 11:6

May

1	2	3	4	5	6
7	8	9	10	11	12	13
14	15	16	17	18	19	20
21	22	23	24	25	26	27
28	29	30	31			

MONDAY 1

Menu:

TUESDAY 2

Menu:

WEDNESDAY 3

Menu:

THURSDAY 4

Menu:

FRIDAY 5

Menu:

SATURDAY 6

Menu:

SUNDAY 7

Menu:

T A S K S L I S T

May 8 - May 14

Strength and honour are her clothing;
and she shall rejoice in time to come.
PROVERBS 31:25

	1	2	3	4	5	6	*May*
7	8	9	10	11	12	13	
14	15	16	17	18	19	20	
21	22	23	24	25	26	27	
28	29	30	31				

MONDAY 8

Menu:

TUESDAY 9

Menu:

WEDNESDAY 10

Menu:

THURSDAY 11

Menu:

FRIDAY 12

Menu:

SATURDAY 13

Menu:

SUNDAY 14

MOTHER'S DAY

Menu:

TASKS LIST

May 15 - May 21

Sow to yourselves in righteousness, reap in mercy; break up your fallow ground: for it is time to seek the LORD, till he come and rain righteousness upon you.
HOSEA 10:12

	1	2	3	4	5	6	May
7	8	9	10	11	12	13	
14	15	16	17	18	19	20	
21	22	23	24	25	26	27	
28	29	30	31				

MONDAY 15

Menu:

TUESDAY 16

Menu:

Cut here

WEDNESDAY 17

Menu:

THURSDAY 18

Menu:

FRIDAY 19

Menu:

SATURDAY 20

Menu:

SUNDAY 21

Menu:

TASKS LIST

May 22 - May 28

A time to be born, and a time to die; a
time to plant, and a time to pluck up
that which is planted.
ECCLESIASTES 3:2

	1	2	3	4	5	6	*May*
7	8	9	10	11	12	13	
14	15	16	17	18	19	20	
21	22	23	24	25	26	27	
28	29	30	31				

MONDAY 22

Menu:

TUESDAY 23

Menu:

WEDNESDAY 24

Menu:

THURSDAY 25

Menu:

FRIDAY 26

Menu:

SATURDAY 27

SUNDAY 28

Menu:

Menu:

Cut here

TASKS LIST

May 29 - June 4

Therefore we ought to give the more earnest
heed to the things which we have heard, lest
at any time we should let them slip.
HEBREWS 2:1

		1	2	3	4	5	6	*May*
7	8	9	10	11	12	13	
14	15	16	17	18	19	20	
21	22	23	24	25	26	27	
28	29	30	31	*1*	*2*	*3*	
4							

MONDAY 29

MEMORIAL DAY

Menu:

TUESDAY 30

Menu:

WEDNESDAY 31

Menu:

THURSDAY 1

Menu:

FRIDAY 2

Menu:

SATURDAY 3

Menu:

SUNDAY 4

Menu:

Cut here

TASKS LIST

WEEK: 23

June 5 - June 11

See then that ye walk circumspectly, not
as fools, but as wise, redeeming the time,
because the days are evil.
EPHESIANS 5:15,16

			1	2	3
4	5	6	7	8	9	10
11	12	13	14	15	16	17
18	19	20	21	22	23	24
25	26	27	28	29	30

June

MONDAY 5

Menu:

TUESDAY 6

Menu:

WEDNESDAY 7

Menu:

THURSDAY 8

Menu:

FRIDAY 9

Menu:

SATURDAY 10

Menu:

SUNDAY 11

Menu:

Cut here

June 12 - June 18

And who knoweth whether thou art come
to the kingdom for such a time as this?
ESTHER 4:14

				1	2	3
4	5	6	7	8	9	10
11	12	13	14	15	16	17
18	19	20	21	22	23	24
25	26	27	28	29	30	

June

MONDAY 12

Menu:

TUESDAY 13

Menu:

WEDNESDAY 14

Menu:

THURSDAY 15

Menu:

FRIDAY 16

Menu:

SATURDAY 17

Menu:

SUNDAY 18

FATHER'S DAY

Menu:

TASKS LIST

June 19 - June 25

The LORD knoweth the days of the upright:
and their inheritance shall be for ever.
They shall not be ashamed in the evil time.
PSALM 37:18,19

				1	2	3
4	5	6	7	8	9	10
11	12	13	14	15	16	17
18	19	20	21	22	23	24
25	26	27	28	29	30	

June

MONDAY 19

Menu:

TUESDAY 20

Menu:

WEDNESDAY 21

Menu:

THURSDAY 22

Menu:

FRIDAY 23

Menu:

SATURDAY 24

Menu:

SUNDAY 25

Menu:

June 26 - July 2

> Thus saith the LORD, In an acceptable
> time have I heard thee, and in a day of
> salvation have I helped thee.
> ISAIAH 49:8

				1	2	3
4	5	6	7	8	9	10
11	12	13	14	15	16	17
18	19	20	21	22	23	24
25	26	27	28	29	30	1
2						

June

MONDAY 26

Menu:

TUESDAY 27

Menu:

WEDNESDAY 28

Menu:

THURSDAY 29

Menu:

FRIDAY 30

Menu:

SATURDAY 1

SUNDAY 2

Menu:

Menu:

T A S K S   L I S T

July 3 - July 9

Walk in wisdom toward them that are
without, redeeming the time.
COLOSSIANS 4:5

						1	July
2	3	4	5	6	7	8	
9	10	11	12	13	14	15	
16	17	18	19	20	21	22	
23	24	25	26	27	28	29	
30	31						

MONDAY 3

Menu:

TUESDAY 4

INDEPENDENCE DAY

Menu:

WEDNESDAY 5

Menu:

THURSDAY 6

Menu:

FRIDAY 7

Menu:

SATURDAY 8

SUNDAY 9

Menu:

Menu:

Cut here

T A S K S   L I S T

July 10 - July 16

Cast thy bread upon the waters: for thou
shalt find it after many days.
ECCLESIASTES 11:1

July

						1
2	3	4	5	6	7	8
9	10	11	12	13	14	15
16	17	18	19	20	21	22
23	24	25	26	27	28	29
30	31					

MONDAY 10

Menu:

TUESDAY 11

Menu:

WEDNESDAY 12

Menu:

THURSDAY 13

Menu:

FRIDAY 14

Menu:

SATURDAY 15

Menu:

SUNDAY 16

Menu:

T A S K S   L I S T

July 17 - July 23

So Christ was once offered to bear the sins
of many; and unto them that look for him
shall he appear the second time without sin
unto salvation.
HEBREWS 9:28

						1
2	3	4	5	6	7	8
9	10	11	12	13	14	15
16	17	18	19	20	21	22
23	24	25	26	27	28	29
30	31					

July

MONDAY 17

Menu:

TUESDAY 18

Menu:

WEDNESDAY 19

Martha Brubacher) 8:30
Carolyn Martin 2:15

Menu:

THURSDAY 20

Menu:

FRIDAY 21

Green Dragon 5:30

Menu:

SATURDAY 22

Menu:

SUNDAY 23

Menu:

T A S K S   L I S T

July 24 - July 30

Humble yourselves therefore under the
mighty hand of God, that he may exalt
you in due time.
1 PETER 5:6

						1
2	3	4	5	6	7	8
9	10	11	12	13	14	15
16	17	18	19	20	21	22
23	24	25	26	27	28	29
30	31					

MONDAY 24

Menu:

TUESDAY 25

Menu:

WEDNESDAY 26

Menu:

THURSDAY 27

Menu:

FRIDAY 28

Menu:

SATURDAY 29

SUNDAY 30

Menu:

Menu:

Cut here

TASKS LIST

July 31 - Aug. 6

For I reckon that the sufferings of this present time are not worthy to be compared with the glory which shall be revealed in us.

ROMANS 8:18

August					
31	1	2	3	4	5
6	7	8	9	10	11	12
13	14	15	16	17	18	19
20	21	22	23	24	25	26
27	28	29	30	31		

MONDAY 31

Menu:

TUESDAY 1

Menu:

WEDNESDAY 2

Menu:

THURSDAY 3

Menu:

FRIDAY 4

Menu:

SATURDAY 5

SUNDAY 6

Menu:

Menu:

Aug. 7 - Aug. 13

For in the time of trouble he shall hide me in
his pavilion: in the secret of his tabernacle shall
he hide me; he shall set me up upon a rock.
PSALM 27:5

	1	2	3	4	5
6	7	8	9	10	11	12
13	14	15	16	17	18	19
20	21	22	23	24	25	26
27	28	29	30	31		

August

MONDAY 7

Menu:

TUESDAY 8

Menu:

WEDNESDAY 9

Menu:

THURSDAY 10

Menu:

FRIDAY 11

Menu:

SATURDAY 12

Menu:

SUNDAY 13

Menu:

TASKS LIST

Aug. 14 - Aug. 20

For when we were yet without strength,
in due time Christ died for the ungodly.
ROMANS 5:6

			1	2	3	4	5
6	7	8	9	10	11	12	
13	14	15	16	17	18	19	
20	21	22	23	24	25	26	
27	28	29	30	31			

August

MONDAY 14

Menu:

TUESDAY 15

Menu:

WEDNESDAY 16

Menu:

THURSDAY 17

Menu:

FRIDAY 18

Menu:

SATURDAY 19

Menu:

SUNDAY 20

Menu:

T A S K S   L I S T

Aug. 21 - Aug. 27

LORD, make me to know mine end, and
the measure of my days, what it is; that I
may know how frail I am.
PSALM 39:4

		1	2	3	4	5
6	7	8	9	10	11	12
13	14	15	16	17	18	19
20	21	22	23	24	25	26
27	28	29	30	31		

August

MONDAY 21

Menu:

TUESDAY 22

Menu:

WEDNESDAY 23

Menu:

THURSDAY 24

Menu:

FRIDAY 25

Menu:

SATURDAY 26

SUNDAY 27

Menu:

Menu:

TASKS LIST

Aug. 28 - Sept. 3

Thy word is true from the beginning: and
every one of thy righteous judgments
endureth for ever.
PSALM 119:160

	1	2	3	4	5	August
6	7	8	9	10	11	12
13	14	15	16	17	18	19
20	21	22	23	24	25	26
27	28	29	30	31	1	2
3						

MONDAY 28

Menu:

TUESDAY 29

Menu:

Cut here

WEDNESDAY 30

Menu:

THURSDAY 31

Menu:

FRIDAY 1

Menu:

SATURDAY 2

Menu:

SUNDAY 3

Menu:

TASKS LIST

Sept. 4 - Sept. 10

Reminder: Your 2018 Planner is available. *See order form in back*

Blessed be the name of God for ever and ever: for wisdom and might are his: and he changeth the times and the seasons: he removeth kings, and setteth up kings: he giveth wisdom unto the wise, and knowledge to them that know understanding.

DANIEL 2:20,21

September

					1	2
3	4	5	6	7	8	9
10	11	12	13	14	15	16
17	18	19	20	21	22	23
24	25	26	27	28	29	30

MONDAY 4

LABOR DAY

Menu:

TUESDAY 5

Menu:

WEDNESDAY 6

Menu:

THURSDAY 7

Menu:

FRIDAY 8

Menu:

SATURDAY 9

Menu:

SUNDAY 10

Menu:

Sept. 11 - Sept. 17

The **LORD** shall preserve thy going out
and thy coming in from this time forth,
and even for evermore.
PSALM 121:8

					1	2
3	4	5	6	7	8	9
10	11	12	13	14	15	16
17	18	19	20	21	22	23
24	25	26	27	28	29	30

September

MONDAY 11

Menu:

TUESDAY 12

Menu:

WEDNESDAY 13

Menu:

THURSDAY 14

Menu:

FRIDAY 15

Menu:

SATURDAY 16

SUNDAY 17

Menu:

Menu:

Cut here

Sept. 18 - Sept. 24

Watch therefore: for ye know not what hour your Lord doth come.
MATTHEW 24:42

						1	2
3	4	5	6	7	8	9	
10	11	12	13	14	15	16	
17	18	19	20	21	22	23	
24	25	26	27	28	29	30	

September

MONDAY 18

Menu:

TUESDAY 19

Menu:

WEDNESDAY 20

Menu:

THURSDAY 21

Menu:

FRIDAY 22

Menu:

SATURDAY 23

SUNDAY 24

Menu:

Menu:

Cut here

TASKS LIST

Sept. 25 - Oct. 1

Whoso keepeth the commandment shall
feel no evil thing: and a wise man's heart
discerneth both time and judgment.
ECCLESIASTES 8:5

September

					1	2
3	4	5	6	7	8	9
10	11	12	13	14	15	16
17	18	19	20	21	22	23
24	25	26	27	28	29	30
1						

MONDAY 25

Menu:

TUESDAY 26

Menu:

WEDNESDAY 27

Menu:

THURSDAY 28

Menu:

FRIDAY 29

Menu:

SATURDAY 30

SUNDAY 1

Menu:

Menu:

TASKS LIST

Oct. 2 - Oct. 8

Let us therefore come boldly unto the
throne of grace, that we may obtain mercy,
and find grace to help in time of need.
HEBREWS 4:16

October						
1	2	3	4	5	6	7
8	9	10	11	12	13	14
15	16	17	18	19	20	21
22	23	24	25	26	27	28
29	30	31				

MONDAY 2

Menu:

TUESDAY 3

Menu:

Cut here

WEDNESDAY 4

Menu:

THURSDAY 5

Menu:

FRIDAY 6

Menu:

SATURDAY 7

Menu:

SUNDAY 8

Menu:

TASKS LIST

Oct. 9 - Oct. 15

For this shall every one that is godly pray
unto thee in a time when thou mayest be
found: surely in the floods of great waters
they shall not come nigh unto him.
PSALM 32:6

1	2	3	4	5	6	7	
8	9	10	11	12	13	14	October
15	16	17	18	19	20	21	
22	23	24	25	26	27	28	
29	30	31					

MONDAY 9

COLUMBUS DAY

Menu:

TUESDAY 10

Menu:

WEDNESDAY 11

Menu:

THURSDAY 12

Menu:

FRIDAY 13

Menu:

SATURDAY 14

Menu:

SUNDAY 15

Menu:

TASKS LIST

Oct. 16 - Oct. 22

Blessed is he that considereth the poor:
the LORD will deliver him in time of
trouble.
PSALM 41:1

1	2	3	4	5	6	7	*October*
8	9	10	11	12	13	14	
15	16	17	18	19	20	21	
22	23	24	25	26	27	28	
29	30	31					

MONDAY 16

Menu:

TUESDAY 17

Menu:

WEDNESDAY 18

Menu:

THURSDAY 19

Menu:

FRIDAY 20

Menu:

SATURDAY 21

Menu:

SUNDAY 22

Menu:

TASKS LIST

Oct. 23 - Oct. 29

What time I am afraid, I will trust in
thee. In God I will praise his word, in God
I have put my trust.

PSALM 56:3,4

1	2	3	4	5	6	7
8	9	10	11	12	13	14
15	16	17	18	19	20	21
22	23	24	25	26	27	28
29	30	31				

October

MONDAY 23

Menu:

TUESDAY 24

Menu:

WEDNESDAY 25

Menu:

THURSDAY 26

Menu:

FRIDAY 27

Menu:

SATURDAY 28

Menu:

SUNDAY 29

Menu:

Oct. 30 - Nov. 5

The night is far spent, the day is at hand: let
us therefore cast off the works of darkness,
and let us put on the armour of light.
ROMANS 13:12

							October
1	2	3	4	5	6	7	
8	9	10	11	12	13	14	
15	16	17	18	19	20	21	
22	23	24	25	26	27	28	
29	30	31	1	2	3	4	
5							

MONDAY 30

Menu:

TUESDAY 31

Menu:

Cut here

WEDNESDAY 1

Menu:

THURSDAY 2

Menu:

FRIDAY 3

Menu:

SATURDAY 4

Menu:

SUNDAY 5

DAYLIGHT SAVINGS TIME ENDS

Menu:

TASKS LIST

Nov. 6 - Nov. 12

Cast me not off in the time of old age;
forsake me not when my strength faileth.
PSALM 71:9

				1	2	3	4
5	6	7	8	9	10	11
12	13	14	15	16	17	18
19	20	21	22	23	24	25
26	27	28	29	30		

November

MONDAY 6

Menu:

TUESDAY 7

Menu:

WEDNESDAY 8

Menu:

THURSDAY 9

Menu:

FRIDAY 10

Menu:

SATURDAY 11

SUNDAY 12

VETERAN'S DAY

Menu:

Menu:

TASKS LIST

Nov. 13 - Nov. 19

Blessed be the name of the LORD from this
time forth and for evermore.
PSALM 113:2

			1	2	3	4
5	6	7	8	9	10	11
12	13	14	15	16	17	18
19	20	21	22	23	24	25
26	27	28	29	30		

November

MONDAY 13

Menu:

TUESDAY 14

Menu:

WEDNESDAY 15

Menu:

THURSDAY 16

Menu:

FRIDAY 17

Menu:

SATURDAY 18

SUNDAY 19

Menu:

Menu:

T A S K S   L I S T

Nov. 20 - Nov. 26

But we will bless the LORD from this
time forth and for evermore.
Praise the LORD.
PSALM 115:18

November
          1   2   3   4
  5   6   7   8   9 10 11
 12 13 14 15 16 17 18
 19 20 21 22 23 24 25
 26 27 28 29 30

MONDAY 20

Menu:

TUESDAY 21

Menu:

WEDNESDAY 22

Menu:

THURSDAY 23

THANKSGIVING

Menu:

FRIDAY 24

Menu:

SATURDAY 25

SUNDAY 26

Menu:

Menu:

TASKS LIST

Nov. 27 - Dec. 3

Whereas ye know not what shall be on the
morrow... For that ye ought to say, If the
Lord will, we shall live, and do this, or that.
JAMES 4:14A-15

			1	2	3	4
5	6	7	8	9	10	11
12	13	14	15	16	17	18
19	20	21	22	23	24	25
26	27	28	29	30	1	2
3						

November

MONDAY 27

Menu:

TUESDAY 28

Menu:

WEDNESDAY 29

Menu:

THURSDAY 30

Menu:

FRIDAY 1

Menu:

SATURDAY 2

Menu:

SUNDAY 3

Menu:

TASKS LIST

Dec. 4 - Dec. 10

Boast not thyself of to morrow; for thou
knowest not what a day may bring forth.
PROVERBS 27:1

					1	2
3	4	5	6	7	8	9
10	11	12	13	14	15	16
17	18	19	20	21	22	23
24	25	26	27	28	29	30
31						

December

MONDAY 4

Menu:

TUESDAY 5

Menu:

WEDNESDAY 6

Menu:

THURSDAY 7

Menu:

FRIDAY 8

Menu:

SATURDAY 9

Menu:

SUNDAY 10

Menu:

Dec. 11 - Dec. 17

Wherefore, if God so clothe the grass of the field, which to day is, and to morrow is cast into the oven, shall he not much more clothe you, O ye of little faith?

MATTHEW 6:30

December

					1	2
3	4	5	6	7	8	9
10	11	12	13	14	15	16
17	18	19	20	21	22	23
24	25	26	27	28	29	30
31						

MONDAY 11

Menu:

TUESDAY 12

Menu:

WEDNESDAY 13

Menu:

THURSDAY 14

Menu:

FRIDAY 15

Menu:

SATURDAY 16

Menu:

SUNDAY 17

Menu:

TASKS LIST

WEEK: 51

I love them that love me; and those
that seek me early shall find me.
PROVERBS 8:17

					1	2
3	4	5	6	7	8	9
10	11	12	13	14	15	16
17	18	19	20	21	22	23
24	25	26	27	28	29	30
31						

December

MONDAY 18

Menu:

TUESDAY 19

Menu:

WEDNESDAY 20

Menu:

THURSDAY 21

Menu:

FRIDAY 22

Menu:

SATURDAY 23

Menu:

SUNDAY 24

CHRISTMAS EVE

Menu:

T A S K S   L I S T

Dec. 25 - Dec. 31

But when the fulness of the time was come, God
sent forth his Son, made of a woman, made under
the law, to redeem them that were under the law,
that we might receive the adoption of sons.
GALATIANS 4:4,5

December

					1	2
3	4	5	6	7	8	9
10	11	12	13	14	15	16
17	18	19	20	21	22	23
24	25	26	27	28	29	30
31						

MONDAY 25

CHRISTMAS DAY

Menu:

TUESDAY 26

Menu:

WEDNESDAY 27

Menu:

THURSDAY 28

Menu:

FRIDAY 29

Menu:

SATURDAY 30

Menu:

SUNDAY 31

NEW YEAR'S EVE

Menu:

TASKS LIST

Jan. 1, 2018 - Jan. 7, 2018

Take therefore no thought for the morrow:
for the morrow shall take thought for the
things of itself. Sufficient unto the day is the
evil thereof.
MATTHEW 6:34

January

	1	2	3	4	5	6
7	8	9	10	11	12	13
14	15	16	17	18	19	20
21	22	23	24	25	26	27
28	29	30	31			

MONDAY 1

NEW YEAR'S DAY

Menu:

TUESDAY 2

Menu:

WEDNESDAY 3

Menu:

THURSDAY 4

Menu:

FRIDAY 5

Menu:

SATURDAY 6

SUNDAY 7

Menu:

Menu:

Cut here

NOTES

Tasks
LIST

We do not
REMEMBER DAYS,
WE REMEMBER
moments.

CESARE PAVESE

Tasks

TASKS LIST

TASKS LIST

TASKS LIST

TASKS LIST

NOTES

Projects
AND EVENTS

Projects

THE BEST

preparation

for tomorrow is doing

YOUR BEST TODAY.

H. JACKSON BROWN, JR.

PROJECTS & EVENTS

PROJECTS & EVENTS

PROJECTS & EVENTS

PROJECTS & EVENTS

PROJECTS & EVENTS

PROJECTS & EVENTS

PROJECTS & EVENTS

PROJECTS & EVENTS

PROJECTS & EVENTS

PROJECTS & EVENTS

PROJECTS & EVENTS

PROJECTS & EVENTS

PROJECTS & EVENTS

NOTES

Information

Remember that
CHILDREN, MARRIAGES,
AND FLOWER GARDENS
reflect the kind of
care
THEY GET.
H. JACKSON BROWN, JR.

NAME	NUMBER	ADDRESS

INFORMATION

NAME	NUMBER	ADDRESS

INFORMATION

NAME	NUMBER	ADDRESS

INFORMATION

NAME	NUMBER	ADDRESS

INFORMATION

NAME	NUMBER	ADDRESS

INFORMATION

NAME	NUMBER	ADDRESS

INFORMATION

NAME	NUMBER	ADDRESS

INFORMATION

NOTES

Shopping
LISTS

Compliment
three people
EVERY DAY.
H. JACKSON BROWN, JR.

STORE PHONE NUMBERS

Shopping

SHOPPING LIST

SHOPPING LIST

SHOPPING LIST

SHOPPING LIST

SHOPPING LIST

SHOPPING LIST

SHOPPING LIST	SHOPPING LIST	SHOPPING LIST

SHOPPING LIST   SHOPPING LIST   SHOPPING LIST

SHOPPING LIST	SHOPPING LIST	SHOPPING LIST

SHOPPING LIST	SHOPPING LIST	SHOPPING LIST

SHOPPING LIST   SHOPPING LIST   SHOPPING LIST

SHOPPING LIST

SHOPPING LIST

SHOPPING LIST

SHOPPING LIST	SHOPPING LIST	SHOPPING LIST

SHOPPING LIST

SHOPPING LIST

SHOPPING LIST

SHOPPING LIST	SHOPPING LIST	SHOPPING LIST

SHOPPING LIST

SHOPPING LIST

SHOPPING LIST

SHOPPING LIST   SHOPPING LIST   SHOPPING LIST

SHOPPING LIST | SHOPPING LIST | SHOPPING LIST

SHOPPING LIST

SHOPPING LIST

SHOPPING LIST

SHOPPING LIST

SHOPPING LIST

SHOPPING LIST

SHOPPING LIST

SHOPPING LIST

SHOPPING LIST

SHOPPING LIST

SHOPPING LIST

SHOPPING LIST

CLOTHING SIZES

CLOTHING SIZES

GIFT IDEAS

MASTER SHOPPING LIST

FRUIT	MEAT	BAKING	BREAKFAST
			PASTA & RICE
VEGETABLES	FROZEN		
		MISCELLANEOUS	BAKERY

MASTER SHOPPING LIST

PERSONAL CARE	CLEANING	SEASONINGS	CANS & JARS

	PAPER PRODUCTS	SAUCES & CONDIMENTS	REFRIGERATED

MEDICATIONS	DRINKS	CHILDCARE	
			ANIMALS

MASTER SHOPPING LIST

FRUIT	MEAT	BAKING	BREAKFAST
			PASTA & RICE
VEGETABLES	FROZEN		
		MISCELLANEOUS	BAKERY

MASTER SHOPPING LIST

PERSONAL CARE	CLEANING	SEASONINGS	CANS & JARS
	PAPER PRODUCTS	SAUCES & CONDIMENTS	REFRIGERATED
MEDICATIONS	DRINKS	CHILDCARE	
			ANIMALS

CHECKLIST FOR _____

_____ _____ _____ _____
_____ _____ _____ _____
_____ _____ _____ _____
_____ _____ _____ _____
_____ _____ _____ _____
_____ _____ _____ _____

CHECKLIST FOR _____

_____ _____ _____ _____
_____ _____ _____ _____
_____ _____ _____ _____
_____ _____ _____ _____
_____ _____ _____ _____
_____ _____ _____ _____

CHECKLIST FOR _____

_____ _____ _____ _____
_____ _____ _____ _____
_____ _____ _____ _____
_____ _____ _____ _____
_____ _____ _____ _____
_____ _____ _____ _____

CHECKLIST FOR _____

_____ _____ _____ _____
_____ _____ _____ _____
_____ _____ _____ _____
_____ _____ _____ _____
_____ _____ _____ _____
_____ _____ _____ _____

CHECKLIST FOR _____

_____ _____ _____ _____
_____ _____ _____ _____
_____ _____ _____ _____
_____ _____ _____ _____
_____ _____ _____ _____
_____ _____ _____ _____

CHECKLIST FOR _____

_____ _____ _____ _____
_____ _____ _____ _____
_____ _____ _____ _____
_____ _____ _____ _____
_____ _____ _____ _____
_____ _____ _____ _____

ORDER FORM

To order, send this completed order form to:

CHRISTIAN LIGHT PUBLICATIONS

P.O. Box 1212 . Harrisonburg, VA 22803-1212

Phone: 1-800-776-0478 • 540-434-1003 • 8:30-5:00 EST

Fax: 540-433-8896 • *E-mail:* orders@clp.com • *Web:* www.clp.org

_____ _____
Name   Date

_____ _____
Mailing Address   Phone

_____ _____
City   State   Zip

2017 Daily Planner Qty. _____ x $14.99 ea. = _____

2018 Daily Planner Qty. _____ x $14.99 ea. = _____

(Prices subject to change without notice)

☐ Check here to receive our free catalog of storybooks, activity books, tracts and more.

Order Summary

Order Subtotal _____ A

5.3% VA Tax (based on A)
(VA residents only) + _____ B

Shipping
• Orders up to $44.50 add $4.00
• Orders $44.51 and over add 9% of A + _____ C

TOTAL of A, B & C _____

All Payments in US Dollars

☐ Check/Money Order   ☐ Visa

☐ MasterCard   ☐ Discover   ☐ American Express

Name on Card _____

_____ - _____ - _____ - _____
Charge Card Number

_____ _____
Exp. Date   Signature

For orders shipping outside the U.S. please call the order department or order online at www.clp.org

Thank you for your order!

thank you

FOR CHOOSING THE

2017 Daily Planner